John Watson Anderson & Minnie Bryan

A Branch of the Anderson Legacy

by

Brian Keith Anderson

1

This book is a work of historical compilation and family preservation. Much of the information within is drawn from public records, genealogy, oral history, and family memory. Every effort has been made to present facts accurately; however, some details may reflect the limitations of available documentation.

Printed in the United States of America

ISBN:9798993853123

DEDICATION

"To John Watson Anderson and Minnie Bryan —

may your footsteps never fade

and your story live as long as ink endures."

With gratitude to Barbara Jo Anderson and Geniel Lee

Anderson, whose visits, kindness, and shared family

Memories helped bring this book to life.

INTRODUCTION

This volume continues the preservation of our family line —

the lives, stories, struggles, and triumphs that formed the roots from

which we now grow.

John Watson Anderson and Minnie Bryan lived in a world far different

from our own, yet the legacy they left still moved within us. Through

land, labor, hardship, faith, and family, they carried forward a story

deserving of light. This book is not merely names and dates — it is the

continuation of memory.

May their lives speak again through these pages.

May this record hold space for those who came before,

and guidance for those who will follow.

— Brian Keith Anderson

TABLE OF CONTENTS

John Watson Anderson & Minnie Bryan
A Branch of the Anderson Legacy

Dedication 3

Introduction 4

Chapter One

The Life of John Watson Anderson 8

Chapter Two

Minnie May Bryan — Her Line, Her People, Her Life 10

Chapter Three

Marriage, Home & the Journey West 17

Chapter Four

The Children of John Watson Anderson & Minnie May Bryan.20

- Alva Lee Anderson
. Jay Anderson
- Wade Anderson

- First Marriage: Edna R. Leduc
- Children of the First Marriage
- Second Marriage: Edna Lola Hannah
- Children of the Second Marriage

Chapter Five

The Parents of John Watson Anderson 56

- Nathaniel Hamilton Anderson
- Sally Adelaide Horton Anderson

Chapter Six

The Anderson Line of Descent 79

- Anders Jöransson
- Ericus Andersson
- Peter Andersson
- Captain John Watson Anderson

Chapter Seven

The Bryan–Meadows Line 87

- James Winton Bryan
- Linnie Bersheba Meadows
- Children of James & Linnie Bryan

Family Memories & Personal Reflections 34

- Geniel Lee Anderson Gibson
- Barbara Jo Anderson
- A Memory from Their Bloodline — Brian Keith Anderson

Epilogue 53

Index 127

CHAPTER ONE

The Life of John Watson Anderson

John Watson Anderson was born on **January 10, 1884**, in **Hillsboro, Coffee County, Tennessee**, a place of rolling hills, quiet farmland, and families rooted deep into Southern earth. He entered life as the son of **Nathaniel Hamilton Anderson**, age **38**, and **Sally Adelaide Horton**, age **39** — mature parents already shaped by the challenges and rhythms of rural Tennessee living.

Late 19th-century Tennessee knew the weight of reconstruction, the ache of old wounds, and the determination of families rebuilding their lives through land, livestock, and labor. Into this landscape came John Watson — a child born into endurance, tradition, and the unspoken expectation to carry the family forward. His childhood would have been marked by seasonal work, church gatherings, small-town life, and the close-knit fabric of a community held together by necessity and faith.

Growing into adulthood, John remained close to the Tennessee soil that raised him. On **November 13, 1908**, at the age of **24**, he married **Minnie May Bryan** in Coffee County. It was the joining of two Southern families — the Andersons and the Bryans — a union that would shape the lineage carried forward in this book. Together, John and Minnie welcomed **three children**, each continuation of their bloodline and story. Life eventually carried John far from the land of his birth. In his later years, he journeyed westward to **Hollister, California**, leaving behind the familiar hills of Tennessee for a distant horizon. There, after 77 years of life, he passed away on **May 2, 1961**. He was laid to rest beneath a California sky — a Tennessee-born man who carried his roots across the country and left them there, planted in new soil.

This book stands as the remembrance of his life —
his beginning in Hillsboro,
his marriage to Minnie,
his children, and their children,
and the legacy still alive today.

A life remembered does not fade. It continues — through us.

CHAPTER TWO

Minnie May Bryan — Her Line, Her People, Her Life

Minnie May Bryan was born in **1888**, a daughter of Tennessee soil, raised in a world of rural families, church pews, and generational continuity. She would one day stand as the matriarch of this branch of the Anderson line — but first, she was simply Minnie, a young woman shaped by the era and the land that bore her.

Details of her early childhood remain scattered through memory and record, yet certain truths defined her youth:

"the rhythm of farm labor, the closeness of family, the expectation of responsibility," from an early age. Girls of her generation learned to cook, to tend the home, to care for siblings, to sew, to carry more weight than their years suggested. Minnie grew strong in that environment — quietly, steadily, without applause.

By **1906**, at around **age 18**, life had already begun to move around her. Tennessee families were expanding, children growing up, marriages forming, land being worked and won. And in the unfolding of time, her

path crossed with that of **John Watson Anderson**.

On **November 13, 1908**, in Coffee County, Tennessee, they were

joined in marriage —

John, age 24,

Minnie, age 20.

Two lives became one story. Together they built a home, raised three

children, stood through years of change, loss, growth, seasons, and

movement. Minnie lived long beyond the early years of their marriage,

reaching the age of **79**, passing from this life in **1967**. Her story did not

end there — it continued in the lives she brought forward.

John Watson Anderson and Minnie May Bryan

John, Minnie and family

John W. Anderson/Spanish American War Veteran

John Watson Anderson and Minnie May Bryan

Jay N., Lawrence Lassiter, Wade, &
Noel Alaqre in front of the
Hollister Chevron Station. They
had this one during the [...]
of the depression.

CHAPTER THREE

Marriage, Home & The Journey West

After their marriage on **November 13, 1908**, in Coffee County, Tennessee, **John Watson Anderson** and **Minnie May Bryan** began their life together in the hills and farmland that had shaped them both. Tennessee was their first home — familiar soil, known faces, shared labor. Their early years were spent close to family, tending land, working fields, raising children, and doing what families of that era did best:

survive, build, endure.

Coffee County holds the first trace of their household — the place where their family began, and where the roots of their branch were first sunk into earth. It was here they welcomed children, built routines, and lived the quiet, honest rhythm of early 1900s Southern life.

But time changes lives, and lives shape time.

John's path did not remain in Tennessee.

17

Records show his footsteps carrying him across the country —

first west to Arizona, then later on to Hollister San Benito, California.

Sometime between those transitions, the Anderson family found a

vastly different world from the rolling Tennessee farmland of John's

youth. The journey alone would have been immense, across mountains,

plains, rivers, and unfamiliar towns. Whether they traveled for work,

opportunity, health, or family remains unknown — but they moved,

and movement shaped legacy.

Into **California**, he settle in **San Benito County**, near the town of

Hollister. The hills there are dry, golden, wind-bent — a land both

rough and beautiful, different from Tennessee yet comforting in its

quiet spaces. Here, John lived his final years, far from where he was

born, yet carrying Tennessee inside him always.

On **May 2, 1961**, at the age of **77**, John Watson Anderson died in

Hollister, California, and was buried there — a Tennessee man rooted

finally in Western soil.

A long journey across a lifetime.

A migration of family, memory, and legacy.

From Coffee County to California —

from beginnings to completion.

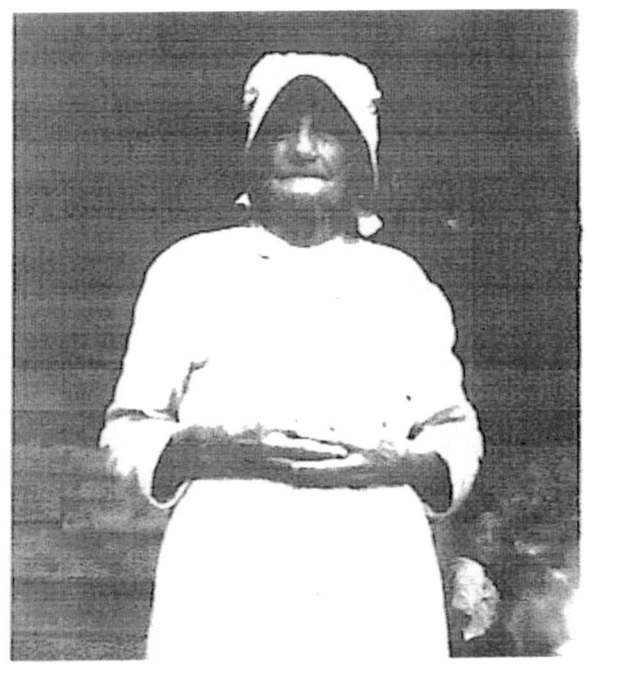

Fanny Pratt delivered: Alva Lee. Jay, and Wade

in Hillsboro Coffee County, Tennessee

CHAPTER FOUR

The Children of John Watson Anderson & Minnie May Bryan

Jay H., Alva Lee, & Frade.
They still lived in
Tenn. when this was
taken.

1. Alva Lee Anderson (Daughter)

Born: *September 5, 1910 · Hillsboro, Coffee County, Tennessee*

Died: *September 5, 1995 · Hollister, San Benito County, California*

Age: *85 years · Born and passed on the same date*

Alva Lee Anderson, **the first born and only daughter** of **John Watson Anderson & Minnie May Bryan**, entered the world in the Tennessee hills on **September 5, 1910**, in **Hillsboro, Coffee County**. As the eldest child — and the only girl "among three children. Alva carried…" a gentle but key role inside the home. Daughters of her era often helped raise younger siblings, learned the rhythm of keeping a household, and formed the emotional center around which family life often revolved.

Her life, like her brothers, would eventually take her far from the soil she was born into. Alva lived to the remarkable age of **85**, passing away on **September 5, 1995**, in **Hollister, California** — the very same day of the year she was born. A perfect circle of life completed, beginning and ending on the same date, separated only by eight and a half decades of living, loving, and legacy.

From Tennessee birth to California rest —

Alva carried the family forward as the Anderson daughter,

a balancing presence between two brothers and a pioneering generation.

Alva Lee Anderson & Barbara Jo

Alva Lee and Jay Anderson

2. John W. "Jay" Anderson

23

Born: *April 13, 1912 · Hillsboro, Coffee County, Tennessee*

Died: *April 14, 1988 · San Jose, Santa Clara County, California*

Age: *76 years*

John W. Anderson — known to family as **"Jay"** — was born on **April 13, 1912**, just two years after his sister, Alva. Like his parents and older brother, he entered life in **Hillsboro, Coffee County, Tennessee**, surrounded by fields, family, and the steady pace of early 20th-century rural life.

Jay's path would eventually follow the westward trail established by the Anderson family. He carried Tennessee roots into new landscapes, living his later years not in the place of his birth, but in the modern and growing world of **San Jose, California**. There he lived his last chapter, passing away on **April 14, 1988**, one day after his 76th birthday.

Another Anderson born in Tennessee —
another life that ended beneath Western skies.

Two sons, two lives carried from the hills of Coffee County
to the valleys and cities of California.

A family migrating with time.

Wade in Tenn. Wade in Tenn.

3. Wade Anderson

Born: *December 12, 1913 · Hillsboro, Coffee County, Tennessee*

Died: *January 31, 1987 · San Benito County, California*

Age: *73 years*

The youngest child of **John Watson Anderson** and **Minnie May Bryan**, **Wade Anderson** was born **December 12, 1913**, again in the familiar hills of **Hillsboro, Coffee County, Tennessee** — the same land that cradled the birth of his two older brothers.

Wade grew up as the third and final son in a family rooted deeply in Southern tradition, faith, and resilience. Like his brothers before him, his path eventually turned westward, following the family migration that carried the Anderson name across the continent.

He passed away on **January 31, 1987**, in **San Benito County, California** — the same region where both his father and brother's journeys concluded. Tennessee was where his life began, but California was where it settled, finished, and returned into memory.

Two brothers and one sister brothers — all born in Tennessee,

all eventually resting in the West.

A full arc of migration, of movement, of legacy carried forward.

"First Wife of Wade Anderson"

Edna R. Leduc

Birth: 17 JUL 1917 • Kings, California

Death: 8 SEPT 2018 • David City, Kansas

Narrative:

Edna R. Leduc was the first wife of Wade Anderson and the mother of their daughter, Barbara Jo Anderson. Born in Kings County, California, Edna lived more than a century before passing in David City, Kansas. Through Barbara—and her connection to Wade's branch of the family—Edna's place in the Anderson legacy remains meaningful and enduring.

"Children of the First Marriage"

Barbara Jo Anderson & Eddie her brother

Birth: 29 AUG 1935 • San Benito, California

Death: Living

Narrative:

Barbara Jo Anderson is the daughter of Wade Anderson and his first wife, Edna R. Leduc. Born in San Benito County, California in 1935, Barbara carries forward this branch of the Anderson family line. Her memories, stories, and kindness have contributed to preserving the legacy of her father's generation.

Child of the First Marriage

Edward J. Anderson

Birth: 6 DEC 1936 • San Benito, California

Death: 27 DEC 2023 Missouri Valley, Iowa

Narrative:

Edward J. Anderson is the son of Wade Anderson and his first wife, Edna R. Leduc. Born in San Benito County, California in 1936, Edward represents the second child of this marriage. His life continues the California branch of the Anderson family line, linking back to both his parents and the larger Anderson legacy.

"Second Wife of Wade Anderson"

Edna Lola Hannah

Birth: 19 DEC 1924 • California, United States

Death: 5 APR 1999 • California, United States

Edna Hannah

Narrative:

Edna Lola Hannah was the second wife of Wade Anderson. Born in California in 1924, she spent her life within the state, passing in 1999. Her marriage to Wade represents the next chapter in his life after his first marriage to Edna R. Leduc. Through her presence and connection to the Anderson line, she remains an important part of Wade's story.

"Children of the Second Marriage"

Geniel Lee Anderson

Birth: 30 OCT 1944 • San Benito, California

Death: Living

Narrative:

Geniel Lee Anderson is the first child of Wade Anderson and his second wife, Edna Lola Hannah. Born in San Benito County, California in 1944, Geniel represents the continuation of Wade's family line through his second marriage. Her life and connection to both parents form an important part of this branch of the Anderson legacy.

Child of the Second Marriage

Wade Buford Anderson Jr.

Birth: 20 JAN 1947 • San Benito, California

Death: 29 AUG 2000 • Hollister, San Benito, California, United States of America

Narrative:

Wade Anderson Jr. was the second child of Wade Anderson and his second wife, Edna Lola Hannah. Born in San Benito County, California in 1947, he spent his life within the community that shaped the Anderson family's western branch. He passed away in Hollister in

2000. Through his life and legacy, Wade Jr. carries forward the Anderson name and the generational story of this line.

Child of the Second Marriage

Gary Leon Anderson

Birth: 1 JUNE 1949 • San Benito, California

Death: 15 AUG 2010 • Apache Junction, Maricopa County, Arizona, USA

Narrative:

Gary Leon Anderson was the third child of Wade Anderson and his second wife, Edna Lola Hannah. Born in San Benito County, California in 1949, Gary later made his home in Arizona, where he passed away in 2010. His life story represents another branch of Wade Anderson's western lineage, extending the Anderson legacy beyond California into the desert Southwest.

Family Memories

Shared by Granddaughter Geniel Lee Anderson

Geniel and Barbara's Memorie's

He was a man of very few words — quiet in nature, reserved, but not easily forgotten. One of Geniel's earliest memories was visiting him near Watsonville, California. He was managing an orchard there — she believes it may have been walnuts — and what stayed with her all these years was how **corn grew between the rows of trees.** As a child, she found that unusual and clever, and sometimes it is those trivial details that imprint a lifetime.

She remembers the **long front porch**, where family sat visiting while she and her brothers **rode his old horse** in the yard. But like most good childhood stories, there was one rule:

"Stay out of the barn."

Why the barn was off-limits is a mystery that still lingers — a thread of curiosity stretching over the years.

Later in life, illness brought him to live with their family. He was a heavy smoker, his legs weak from poor circulation, making walking difficult. Yet despite the struggle, he became a companion to the children after school — playing **checkers, puzzles, chess, Chinese checkers, and cards.** Those simple hours together built a bond without needing many words.

He later stayed with **Uncle J**, then finally with a retired nurse who cared for him through his last days. What Geniel remembers most is his **competitive spirit**, his love for **baseball and fast cars**, and how much he enjoyed **a good game** with anyone willing to sit across the board.

Quiet men speak loudly through memory — and hers has kept him alive all these years.

Geniel Anderson Hodges Gibson

Bill, Danielle, Geniel and Brian, her 80 Birthday

36

Memories of : Barbara Jo Anderson

(From her personal recollections)

A Memory Tribute

Barbara Jo Anderson, daughter of **Wade Buford Anderson Sr.**, recalls her grandparents with warm fragments of memory that have stayed with her through the years — moments small in time, but large in meaning.

"I'm not sure how much I can contribute — Geniel probably has more memories than I do."

Her parents divorced when she was just five, so her time with the Anderson side of the family was scattered — visits when she could, then later moving back at seventeen for a short while before life carried her onward to Los Angeles. Yet even brief moments leave a mark, and Barbara still carries pieces of John W. and Minnie that time could not erase.

Her strongest memories are in Minnie's kitchen.

Minnie cooked **chitlins**, and every holiday she made **pecan pies —
often baking a whole one just for Barbara alone.** A child never
forgets that kind of love. She remembers **drinking coffee from a
saucer**, the old-fashioned way — a small ritual, now a treasure.

Grandpa John Watson, I remember less, but clearly enough to paint a
picture:

Around age seven or eight, Barbara visited him in **Watsonville,
California**, where he worked on an apple farm. That memory sits
beside another, years later — a phone call said that he was in the
hospital, extremely sick. She was in her twenties when she visited him
then. He recovered and eventually lived in **San Jose** with a family who
cared for him in their home.

"Elder care was different then," she recalls.
Instead of nursing homes, families often took elders in.
John W. lived with a **retired nurse and her family — children
included — who loved him and cared for him like one of their own.**

Because of distance and those tender family circumstances, Barbara did not share many holidays or Christmases with the Anderson side. Yet what she does remember shines brightly:

Minnie sewed.

For Barbara — and later for Barbara's children — stitching clothing with her hands, her time, and her heart. When Minnie passed, Barbara felt something awaken in her — a desire to learn to sew as her grandmother once did. And she did.

"I may not have many stories, but I hope this helps."

Barbara still has photographs — even one of **the only car Minnie ever drove**, a priceless piece of Anderson history. She has offered to share copies for the book.

Barbara Jo Anderson

Barbara Jo and George Gibson d. Aug. 4, 2021

A Memory From Their Bloodline — By

Brian Keith Anderson

Anderson Family Reunion
June 16, 2018
Hillsboro, Tennessee

Wilson Bedwell Photography

"I remember the Anderson reunions — the sound of family laughter, potluck tables long enough to stretch across generations, and stories that traveled from mouth to mouth like shared inheritance.

I did not grow up knowing every detail of their lives, but I felt them —

in the faces of cousins, in the warmth of gathering, in the way family

finds its way back home.

John W. and Minnie were more than names written in records. They

were roots. And every time we met under those old trees, their legacy

lived again."

Brian Keith Anderson Jan. 7, 1958

Personal Note:

Finding **Barbara and Geniel** was a high point for me at that time. Growing up, I have heard stories about **John W. Anderson** and **Minnie Bryan**, and I often wondered who they truly were and what their lives had been like. I was told that John W. Anderson— grandson of **Captain John W. Anderson**—had been caught making whiskey. To avoid prosecution, he took his family and fled across the Tennessee state line. Their journey carried them west to **Arizona**, and eventually they settled in **Hollister, California**. There, John W. Anderson lived and worked on an **apple orchard farm**, building a new life for his family far from their Tennessee roots. Later in my life, I traveled to **Hollister, California**, determined to find where **John W. Anderson** and **Minnie Bryan Anderson** had been laid to rest. Standing there, I located their graves and took photographs, finally putting faces and places to the names that had followed me since childhood. In that quiet moment, the stories I had heard for years felt real and grounded in history.

There, in Hollister, I found **John W. and Minnie**, along with other members of the family, all buried in the same place. Seeing their names carved in stone brought a sense of closure and connection. It felt as though a long journey—one that had begun generations earlier in Tennessee—had finally come full circle. By finding them, I was not only honoring their lives but also preserving their memory for future generations of our family.

Standing in that cemetery in **Hollister, California**, I felt a quiet stillness settle around me. The journey that had carried **John W. Anderson** and **Minnie Bryan Anderson** so far from Tennessee had ended there, beneath the same California sky they had chosen for their new beginning. What once had been only stories passed down through family conversations now rested in front of me, marked in stone.

Finding their graves was more than a research milestone—it was personal. It connected generations that had been separated by distance, time, and silence. As I photographed their headstones, I thought about the courage it must have taken to leave everything familiar behind and start again in an unknown land. Their lives spoke of perseverance, sacrifice, and the quiet strength of family.

Nearby were the graves of other family members, all part of the same story. Seeing them together reminded me that no one's journey is walked alone. Each name represented a life lived, choices made, and a place secured in our family's unfolding history. At that moment, I felt a deep responsibility to remember them, to tell their stories with care, and to ensure they were not forgotten.

Walking away from the cemetery, I carried more than photographs with me. I carried a renewed sense of purpose. Their journey had not ended, but it had simply been passed forward. By recording their lives and preserving their memory, I was honoring not only **John and Minnie**, but all those who came before and after them. This, I realized, was the true meaning of legacy.

When I finally met **Geniel**, it was when she came down to **Tennessee** to attend the **Anderson Family Reunions** that I used to organize. She traveled with her husband, **Hoot Gibson**, making the long journey to reconnect with family she had not seen in years.

Her presence felt significant, though at the time I did not realize just how important it would become. Meeting Geniel added a living connection to the stories I had been uncovering—someone who carried memories, relationships, and family history that could not be found in records or documents. Through her, the names in my research gained voices and faces.

That meeting marked another turning point in my journey. What had once been distant history was now personal, shared across a table, in conversations, and in quiet moments of recognition. The family story was no longer just something I was researching, it was something I was living and helping to bring back together.

I showed **Geniel** and **Hoot** all the things I had collected over the years and introduced them to cousins they had never met before. During that visit, we spent time sharing stories, laughing, and connecting pieces of the family that had long been separated. It was a wonderful visit; one filled with a sense of reunion and belonging.

The day before, I had met them for **breakfast at a local restaurant**. Geniel had brought along a photo album—one filled with old family photographs. There were many pictures, some carefully labeled with names and others left unnamed. As we went through them together, I recognized many of the faces from **Tennessee**, having already encountered them during my research into the Anderson family line.

That moment felt especially meaningful. Faces I had only known through records and names in family trees were suddenly real, preserved in photographs and memories. It was the kind of discovery I loved most finding both old and new pictures and watching the past come alive again. It reminded me why preserving these stories matters, and why bringing families back together is worth the effort.

After the reunion the following day, **Geniel and Hoot** came by my house. I still had food left over from the reunion, so we made lunch from what remained and sat together visiting for a while. It was an easy, comfortable time, one of those moments where conversation flows naturally and time seems to slow down.

During our visit, they asked if I would take them to the **old home place where Captain Anderson once lived**. I agreed, and after loading them into my **Blazer**, I drove them out to the site. I was not alone in preparing the place—**Joe Bryan** had cleaned it up months earlier, salvaging some of the wood. From that wood, he later built the bed I sleep on today, giving new life to part of that old home.

When we arrived, the **stone foundation** was still there, resting quietly where the house once stood. One of the **corner stones** remained intact. Geniel picked it up, holding a tangible piece of her family's past, and later took it back with her to **Colorado**. It felt right—like a fragment of history finding its way home with her.

That visit to the old home place carried a deep sense of continuity. Wood, stone, memory, and family had all survived the passing of time, each in its own way. Standing there together, it felt as though the past and present were finally meeting.

I still text **Geniel** and **Barbara** from time to time to check on them and see how they are doing. From the moment we met, they felt like family. There was no hesitation, no distance, just an immediate sense of connection, as if we had known one another all along.

That bond has remained grounded in shared history and mutual respect. What began as research and curiosity grew into something far more meaningful. In reconnecting with them, I gained not only a deeper understanding of our family's past, but also living reminders that family ties endure, no matter how much time or distance separates us.

Sadly, **Hoot Gibson** has passed away by the time I am drafting this book. He was a lot of fun to be around, and whenever I think of him, I still find myself smiling. His presence brought laughter and warmth to every gathering.

His passing has been especially hard on **Geniel**. They were close, and their bond was evident to anyone who knew them. Losing him left a space that can never truly be filled, only carried forward in memory and love.

My prayer is simple and sincere: **God, watch over them**. I hold Geniel, Barbara, and all of our family close in my heart. I love them all, and I am grateful for every moment we were given together.

Geniel trusted me with her photo album, allowing me to keep it long enough to copy every picture and save them to my computer. Once I carefully preserved the images, I returned the album to her. Those photographs became an important part of this book, helping ensure that the faces and memories they contained would be protected for future generations.

When I began drafting this book, I asked **Geniel and Barbara** if they would write something so I could include their words as part of the story and as a dedication to them. I was deeply grateful when they agreed. Their contributions added voices that no document or record could ever replace.

Because of this book, they—and the generations before them—will not be forgotten. Their stories now stand alongside their ancestors, preserved together in one place, bound by memory, history, and love.

Dedication

This section of the book is dedicated to **Geniel Lee Anderson Gibson** and **Barbara Jo Anderson**.

Your willingness to share your memories, your photographs, and your voices has helped preserve a part of our family's history that might otherwise have been lost to time. Through your contributions, names became faces, and stories once spoken quietly were given a place to rest and be remembered.

May these pages honor not only your lives, but also the generations who came before you. Your place within this family story is secure, now and for those yet to come.

With gratitude, respect, and love.

Editor's Note

Geniel Lee Anderson Gibson and Barbara Jo Anderson generously provided the following written reflections. Their words are presented with care and minimal editing, preserving their voices as they were shared with me.

These personal recollections add depth and humanity to the historical record, offering perspectives that no document or archive could fully capture. Together, their contributions bridge the past and the present, ensuring that lived experience stands alongside genealogy in telling our family's story.

Epilogue

Family history is more than dates, places, and records—it is carried in memories, relationships, and the quiet moments that connect one generation to the next. Through this journey of discovery, what began as research became reunion, and what began as questions became connection.

The stories of **John W. Anderson** and **Minnie Bryan Anderson** traveled far—from Tennessee to the western edge of the country—and yet their legacy never truly left home. It lived on in their descendants, waiting for the right time to be rediscovered and remembered.

By gathering these stories, photographs, and voices together, this chapter closes not with an ending, but with continuity. The past has been honored, the present acknowledged, and the future given a foundation. In this way, the family story carries on—remembered, preserved, and never forgotten.

Every generation has one individual whose life becomes the anchor for the stories that follow. For the Anderson family line, that person was **John Watson Anderson**, born into a world shaped by the resilience of his parents, **Nathaniel Hamilton Anderson,** and **Sally Adelaide Horton Anderson**, and strengthened by the traditions of rural Coffee County, Tennessee.

John W.'s childhood unfolded against the backdrop of hills, farms, and simple community life — a place where demanding work was expected, and family ties ran deep. From an early age he learned the values that would define him: the discipline of labor beside his father, the compassion and steadiness taught by his mother, and the quiet strength that comes from growing up close to the land.

The years of his youth were not easy ones. Tennessee was still healing from the Civil War, and families like the Andersons were rebuilding their lives with determination and faith. Yet these challenges shaped John W. into a young man of character. He grew up watching his father work tirelessly, and he experienced firsthand the sacrifices required to keep a family together during uncertain times.

This chapter begins with his story — not just the events of his life, but the legacy he would carry, strengthen, and pass down. To understand the Anderson line as it stands today, we must begin with the early years of the man whose footsteps still echo through these pages.

Chapter 5:

Introductions to the Parents of John W. Anderson

Father: Nathaniel Hamilton Anderson

Born: 18 June 1845 — Hillsboro, Coffee County, Tennessee

Died: 8 May 1919 — Hillsboro, Coffee County, Tennessee

Nathaniel Hamilton Anderson was the steady cornerstone of the Anderson family line during a period of profound change in Tennessee's history. Born in the hills of Coffee County, his early years were shaped by the rhythm of rural life — hard work, strong family ties, and the demands of the land. He came of age during a turbulent era, witnessing the Civil War sweep through the South and the challenges that followed in the years of rebuilding.

Nathaniel was a man molded by responsibility. He earned his living through labor that required strength, determination, and endurance. Whether it was farming, timber work, or the daily tasks required to

56

keep a household functioning in rural Tennessee, he carried the load with a quiet persistence. His hands built the world his children would grow up in, and his values of honesty, discipline, and loyalty took root in the next generation.

For John W. Anderson, Nathaniel was more than a father — he was a living example of resilience. The lessons learned at Nathaniel's side became the foundation John W. carried into adulthood, shaping his own role as a father, provider, and shaper of the Anderson line.

Mother: Sally Adelaide Horton Anderson

Born: 4 November 1844 — Coffee County, Tennessee

Died: 5 April 1917 — Hillsboro, Coffee County, Tennessee

Sally Adelaide Horton grew up in the same Tennessee hills that shaped generations of families before her. Her early life was guided by the traditions and expectations placed upon women of her time — to keep the home, nurture the children, and steady the family through whatever trials might come.

Sally was known for her quiet resilience. In a world that demanded much from mothers, she provided the emotional center of the Anderson household. Her days were filled with the rhythm of tending to children, managing the home, supporting her husband's work, and holding the family together through seasons of plenty and seasons of hardship.

It was Sally's steadfast presence that shaped the heart of her son, **John W. Anderson**. From her he learned compassion, patience, and the importance of family unity. Her influence can be felt through the generations — in the stories, values, and memories that still linger in the Anderson name.

A Legacy Rooted in Strength

Together, **Nathaniel and Sally** created the environment in which John W. Anderson was raised — a home built on faith, hard work, and family tradition. Their lives formed the deep roots of the Anderson line that continues to this day, and their legacy lives on through the stories preserved in this book.

Nathaniel Hamilton Anderson and Sally Adelaide Horton

Children's:

Sibling 1 — William H. Anderson

Born: March 12, 1870, • Hillsboro, Coffee County, Tennessee

Died: July 11, 1922, • Norman, Cleveland County, Oklahoma

Narrative Paragraph (you can use this or let me adjust it):

William H. Anderson was one of the older sons in the family, born during the years when Joseph and Nancy were still rooted in Hillsboro. Like many Anderson men of his generation, William followed the path of hard work, migration, and building new opportunity as the family began moving westward. His life carried him to Norman, Cleveland County, Oklahoma, where he passed in 1922. His movement mirrors the early beginnings of the Anderson family's transition from Tennessee to the expanding frontier of Oklahoma.

Note: gravestones of W.H, and Venia

Wife of William H. Anderson — Hattie Lavenia Wilson

Born: April 8, 1869, • Hillsboro, Coffee County, Tennessee
Died: January 21, 1936, • Norman, Cleveland County, Oklahoma

Narrative Paragraph:

Hattie Lavenia Wilson married William H. Anderson and journeyed with him through the family's transition from Tennessee to Oklahoma. Born in Hillsboro like many of the Andersons, she shared the same rural upbringing and pioneer spirit that defined the generation. Hattie made her final home in Norman, Cleveland County, where several branches of the Anderson family eventually gathered. Her life stands as a steady presence alongside William during a time of momentous change and movement for the family.

Sibling 2 — Edgar Anderson

Born: January 30, 1871, • Hillsboro, Coffee County, Tennessee

Died: February 4, 1956, • Hillsboro, Coffee County, Tennessee

Tag: *Edgar Anderson — Great-Grandfather of the modern Anderson line.*

Narrative Paragraph:

Edgar Anderson stayed in Hillsboro throughout his life, remaining deeply connected to the family's Tennessee roots. While other brothers and sisters moved west into Oklahoma, Edgar held the original Anderson home ground, carrying forward the traditions of the earlier generations. His long life bridged the pioneer era with the modern family, and his role as a great-grandfather places him at the heart of your lineage.

Wife of Sibling 2 — Harriet E. Jones

Born: March 11, 1873, • Hillsboro, Coffee County, Tennessee

Died: June 22, 1967, • Hillsboro, Coffee County, Tennessee

Tag: *Harriet E. (Jones) Anderson — Great-Grandmother, wife of Edgar Anderson.*

Narrative Paragraph:

Harriet E. Jones married Edgar Anderson and became the matriarch of your great-grandparent generation. Born and raised in Hillsboro, she shared the same deep Tennessee roots as the Anderson family. Harriet lived a long and steady life, witnessing the transitions of the family from the late 1800s through the mid-1900s. Her presence anchored the household Edgar kept in Tennessee, preserving the original Anderson line while other branches moved westward.

Note: I was incredibly young when I first remember Grandee Harriet, she was in the nursing home then. I remember I went to her funeral, but I did not understand what was happening. Everyone was crying and it made me sad and then I started to cry, my dad had me sit with him on the first row. He was a pallbearer.

Staley Bros., Tullahoma, Tenn.

Sibling 3 — Edward Anderson

Born: January 30, 1871, • Hillsboro, Coffee County, Tennessee

Died: November 5, 1929, • Hillsboro, Coffee County, Tennessee

Tag: *Edward Anderson — Great-Granduncle.*

Narrative Paragraph:

Edward Anderson was one of the siblings who, like Edgar, remained rooted in Hillsboro throughout his life. Born into the same close-knit Tennessee household, Edward lived during the years when the Anderson family was beginning to spread across the country. While some siblings migrated west, Edward stayed close to the ancestral home. His life helps complete the picture of the generation that shaped the early Anderson heritage in Coffee County.

Wife of Sibling 3 — Mary Ethel Smythe

Born: August 31, 1886, • Coffee County, Tennessee
Died: May 14, 1967, • Manchester, Coffee County, Tennessee

Tag: *Mary Ethel (Smythe) Anderson — Great-Grandaunt (by marriage), wife of Edward Anderson.*

Narrative Paragraph:

Mary Ethel Smythe married Edward Anderson and became part of the Tennessee branch of the Anderson family. Born in Coffee County, she shared the same hometown roots and traditions as the Andersons. Mary spent her life in the familiar landscapes of Coffee County, eventually settling in Manchester. Through her marriage to Edward, she helped continue the Anderson presence in Tennessee during a time when other family lines were spreading westward.

Sibling 4 — Virginia Pearl Anderson

Born: October 1874 • Hillsboro, Coffee County, Tennessee

Died: February 26, 1910, • Tennessee

Narrative Paragraph:

Virginia Pearl Anderson was one of the younger daughters in the family, born during the later years of Joseph and Nancy's time in Hillsboro. Her life remained centered in Tennessee, where many of the Anderson siblings chose to stay rooted. Virginia Pearl's early passing in 1910 left a quiet but lasting mark on the family, remembered as part of the strong line of Anderson daughters who helped shape the home life and stability of the Tennessee branch.

Husband of Sibling 4 — Charlie Pratt

Born: December 26, 1876, • Hillsboro, Coffee County, Tennessee

Died: November 28, 1954, • Hillsboro, Coffee County, Tennessee

Tag: *Charlie Pratt — Great-Granduncle (by marriage), husband of Virginia Pearl Anderson.*

Narrative Paragraph:

Charlie Pratt married Virginia Pearl Anderson and became part of the Tennessee-rooted branch of the Anderson family. Like the Andersons, he was born in Hillsboro and spent his life in Coffee County, sharing the same rural traditions and community ties. Even after Virginia Pearl's early passing, Charlie continued to represent the steady presence of the extended Anderson family in Hillsboro. His long-life bridged generations and kept the family line connected to its Tennessee homeland.

Luther Nathaniel Anderson and Joe Lusk

Sibling 5 — Luther Nathaniel Anderson

Born: August 23, 1877, • Hillsboro, Coffee County, Tennessee

Died: May 8, 1945, • McMinnville, Warren County, Tennessee

Narrative Paragraph:

Luther Nathaniel Anderson was born during the final years of the family's time in Hillsboro and grew up alongside the younger Anderson siblings. His life carried him into nearby Warren County, where he eventually made his home in McMinnville. Luther represents the branch of the Anderson family that remained within Middle Tennessee, close to their ancestral community. His life reflects the steady continuation of the Anderson name across county lines while maintaining deep roots in the region.

Wife of Sibling 5 — Joseph "Joe" Albert Lusk

Born: October 3, 1880, • Hillsboro, Coffee County, Tennessee

Died: April 15, 1970, • Cannon County, Tennessee

Tag: *Joseph "Joe" Albert Lusk — Great-Grandaunt, wife of Luther Nathaniel Anderson. Named after her father.*

Narrative Paragraph:

Joseph "Joe" Albert Lusk, despite her traditionally masculine name, was the beloved wife of Luther Nathaniel Anderson. She was named after her father, a family detail that carried forward through generations as a point of pride and remembrance. Born in Hillsboro, she shared the same Tennessee roots and heritage as the Anderson family. Joe later lived in Cannon County, where she continued the strong legacy of the Anderson-Lusk connection and remained an anchor for her branch of the family well into 1970.

Sibling 6 — John Watson Anderson

Born: January 10, 1884, • Hillsboro, Coffee County, Tennessee

Died: May 2, 1961, • Hollister, San Benito County, California

Narrative Paragraph:

John Watson Anderson was among the younger sons of Joseph and Nancy, born during the final years of the family's time in Hillsboro. While many Anderson siblings remained in Tennessee or migrated west to Oklahoma, John Watson's path carried him even farther—to California. His move to Hollister in San Benito County reflects the expanding reach of the Anderson family across the country during the early 20th century. John Watson's journey stands as a testament to the spirit of exploration found within this generation of Andersons.

Wife of Sibling 6 — Minnie May Bryan

Born: May 1, 1888, • Hillsboro, Coffee County, Tennessee
Died: March 8, 1967, • Hollister, San Benito County, California

Tag: *Minnie May (Bryan) Anderson — Wife of John Watson Anderson.*

Narrative Paragraph:

Minnie May Bryan was born in Hillsboro, Tennessee, and her life became deeply connected to the Anderson family through her marriage to John Watson Anderson. Together, they formed the branch of the family that journeyed the farthest west, eventually settling in Hollister, California. Minnie remained there throughout her later years, passing away in 1967. Her life beautifully reflects the Anderson story—rooted in Tennessee tradition yet stretching out toward new horizons across the country.

. The deeper roots of the Anderson family—stretching back through generations—are recorded in the **Anderson Legacy** book, where the full ancestral line is preserved in greater detail.

his volume focuses on the life and descendants of **John Watson Anderson**. The broader ancestral history of the Anderson family is docu

The Anderson Line of Descent

The story of **John Watson Anderson** is not a single chapter, but the continuation of a much older journey—one that began across the Atlantic and unfolded through generations of perseverance, migration, and settlement.

Anders Jöransson

The earliest known ancestor of this Anderson line, **Anders Jöransson** lived in Sweden during the 1600s. From him began the family name that would, over time, cross oceans, and continents. His life marks the origin point of a lineage shaped by endurance and movement.

Ericus Andersson (Jöransson)

Son of Anders Jöransson, **Ericus Andersson** carried the family forward during a period when surnames were still evolving. His name appears in historical records under several spellings, reflecting the transition from traditional Scandinavian patronymic naming to more permanent family surnames.

Peter Andersson

As the family migrated toward the Americas, naming conventions continued to shift. **Peter Andersson** represents the bridge between Old World identity and emerging American lineage, standing at the threshold between European origins and life in a new land.

Ericus Anderson

With settlement in America, the surname began to take its Anglicized form. **Ericus Anderson** reflects this transition, as the family name adapted to English-speaking records and customs.

Peter Anderson

By this generation, the **Anderson** surname had fully taken hold. **Peter Anderson** stands among the early American roots of this family line, grounding the name in the soil of a growing nation.

Captain John Watson Anderson

A defining figure in the Anderson legacy, **Captain John Watson Anderson** firmly established the family in Tennessee. Through his leadership, land ownership, and presence in the community, he shaped the direction of generations that followed.

Nathaniel Hamilton Anderson

Son of Captain John Watson Anderson, **Nathaniel Hamilton Anderson** carried the family through the post–Civil War years. His life anchored the Anderson name in **Coffee County, Tennessee**, forming the foundation upon which his children, including **John Watson Anderson**—were raised.

Also, linage is in the **Anderson Legacy** book.

Anders Jöransson

(b. 1645, Sweden – d. 1690, Delaware Colony)

└── Ericus Jöransson Andersson

(b. May 13, 1671, Fort Christina, Delaware – d. March 25, 1765)

|

└── Peter Ericsson Andersson

(b. 1706 – d. 1787)

|

└── Ericus Anderson

(b. 1737 – d. 1811)

|

└── Peter Anderson

(b. 1765 – d. 1824)

|

└── Captain John Watson Anderson

(b. 1806 – d. 1879)

|

└── Nathaniel Hamilton Anderson

(b. 1837 – d. 1919)

|

└── John Watson Anderson

(b.1884 – d. 1961)

Transition into the Bryan–Meadows Line

With the foundation of the Anderson line established, the story now turns to the family of **Minnie May Bryan**, whose life and lineage became inseparably woven into the Anderson legacy through marriage. While the Anderson story traces its roots across oceans and generations, the Bryan–Meadows line speaks of deep Tennessee soil, quiet perseverance, and families whose strength was carried not in titles or land grants, but in daily endurance.

Through Minnie, two family histories meet—one shaped by long migration and settlement, the other by continuity and steadfast presence. Her lineage adds balance to the Anderson narrative, grounding it in the lived experience of rural Middle Tennessee families whose influence flowed forward through home, faith, and kinship.

The pages that follow step into the Bryan–Meadows line not as a departure, but as a continuation—another branch of the same enduring story, shaped by different paths yet bound by the same commitment to family, memory, and legacy.

Minnie May Bryan (b. 1888-d. 1967)

Minnie May Bryan

The Quiet Strength of the Bryan–Meadows Line

Minnie May Bryan was born on **May 1, 1888**, in **Hillsboro, Coffee County, Tennessee**, a place shaped by red clay soil, close-knit families, and the steady rhythm of rural life. She entered the world as the daughter of **James Winton Bryan** and **Linnie Bersheba Meadows**, carrying within her the combined heritage of the Bryan and Meadows families—both deeply rooted in Middle Tennessee.

Minnie's early childhood was lived in the familiar patterns of the late nineteenth century: home, land, church, and kin. Her mother, Linnie Bersheba Meadows, was born in **Grundy County, Tennessee**, on **August 25, 1856**, and brought with her the quiet resilience of mountain families who understood endurance as a way of life. Her father, James Winton Bryan, born **April 2, 1853**, in **Coffee County**, worked the land and carried the responsibilities common to men of his generation—provider, laborer, and anchor to the household.

Tragedy marked Minnie's youth early. On **January 19, 1898**, her mother, Linnie, passed away in **Coffee County**, leaving Minnie motherless at just nine years old. That loss shaped her childhood in ways not recorded in documents but carried forward in character. Children of that era learned quickly to shoulder responsibility, to grow inward strength, and to move forward without complaint. Minnie was one of them.

On **November 13, 1908**, in **Coffee County, Tennessee**, Minnie married **John Watson Anderson**, uniting the Bryan–Meadows line with the Anderson family—a lineage already stretching back generations. Minnie was twenty years old. Together, she and John built a life rooted first in Tennessee and later carried westward across the country. Their union produced children, continuity, and a legacy that would follow them far beyond their birthplace.

As the Anderson family migrated, Minnie's life expanded beyond the familiar hills of Coffee County. She journeyed west with her family, eventually settling in **Hollister, San Benito County, California**.

There, far from the Tennessee soil where she was born, she remained anchored by memory, family, and the values formed in her early years.

Minnie May Bryan Anderson passed away on **March 8, 1967**, in **Hollister, California**. Her life bridged two centuries, two regions of the country, and two-family lines. Though she lived quietly, her influence endured—through the children she raised, the traditions she carried, and the legacy preserved in the generations that followed.

Minnie's story is not one of public records or loud acclaim. It is the story of countless women whose strength lived in homes, whose endurance shaped families, and whose legacy continues not in monuments, but in memory.

James Winton Bryan

A Father Rooted in Coffee County

James Winton Bryan was born on **April 2, 1853**, in **Coffee County,**

Tennessee, during a time when life was measured by seasons, land, and the strength of one's hands. He came of age in the years following the Civil War, a period that demanded resilience from Southern families as they rebuilt lives shaped by loss, labor, and perseverance.

Raised in the familiar hills and valleys of Coffee County, James learned early the responsibilities expected of men in rural Tennessee. Work was not optional, it was survival. The land provided only what was given in effort, and James answered that demand with steadiness rather than ambition. He lived not as a man seeking notice, but as one committed to providing for his household and preserving continuity for the generations that followed.

James married **Linnie Bersheba Meadows**, a woman born in nearby **Grundy County, Tennessee**, whose quiet strength matched his own. Together, they formed a household grounded in faith, routine, and family obligation. Their home would have followed the familiar rhythm of the era—fields worked at daylight, meals prepared with care, and evenings shaped by conversation, rest, and shared labor.

Their daughter, **Minnie May Bryan**, was born on **May 1, 1888**, in Hillsboro. James's role as a father unfolded in a world where affection was often expressed through provision rather than words. He raised Minnie during a time when children were expected to grow into responsibility early, learning self-reliance and endurance by example.

Tragedy struck the Bryan household in **1898**, when Linnie passed away at just forty-one years of age. Minnie was only nine years old. With the loss of his wife, James was left to carry the weight of grief alongside the ongoing responsibility of fatherhood. Such losses were common in the nineteenth century, yet they left marks that were carried quietly, without record, into the fabric of family memory.

James continued his life in **Coffee County**, remaining rooted in the same Tennessee soil that had shaped him from birth. He lived to see his daughter grow into adulthood, marry, and eventually carry the family story westward. Though Minnie's path would lead her far from Tennessee, James remained anchored in the place that had always been home.

On **July 9, 1934**, James Winton Bryan passed away in **Manchester, Coffee County, Tennessee**, closing a life that had spanned eighty-one years of change, endurance, and quiet contribution. He did not leave behind written records or public acclaim—but he left something far more enduring: a lineage carried forward through his daughter, woven into the larger Anderson family legacy.

James Winton Bryan's life reminds us that history is often shaped not by those who stand at the center of events, but by those who hold families together through consistency, work, and presence. His legacy lives on in the generations that followed—steady, grounded, and remembered.

Linnie Bersheba Meadows

Life of Quiet Strength, Lived Too Briefly

Linnie Bersheba Meadows was born on **August 25, 1856**, in **Grundy County, Tennessee**, a region shaped by mountain ridges, hard ground, and families who learned endurance as a way of life. Her early years unfolded in a world where strength was seldom announced and rarely written down—where women carried households forward through steadiness, sacrifice, and faith rather than recognition.

Raised in nineteenth-century Tennessee, Linnie grew up in an era when a woman's influence lived within the home. From an early age, she would have learned the skills necessary to sustain family life: cooking, sewing, tending children, and managing the countless unseen labor that held households together. These were not tasks of choice, but of necessity—and Linnie met them with quiet resolve.

She later married **James Winton Bryan**, joining the Meadows line with the Bryan family of **Coffee County, Tennessee**. Their marriage formed a household grounded in shared work and mutual responsibility, shaped by the rhythms of rural life. Together, they built a home where labor, faith, and family were central—not as ideals, but as daily practice.

On **May 1, 1888**, Linnie gave birth to their daughter, **Minnie May Bryan**, in **Hillsboro, Coffee County**. As a mother, Linnie would have been Minnie's first teacher, shaping her understanding of care, duty, and resilience through example rather than instruction. Though few records remain of those early years, the imprint of a mother's presence is rarely lost.

Linnie's life was cut short far too soon. On **January 19, 1898**, she passed away in **Coffee County, Tennessee**, at just **forty-one years of age**. Minnie was only nine years old. In a time when illness and hardship often arrived without warning, such losses were devastating— and yet endured in silence. Linnie's absence would shape her daughter's childhood profoundly, imprinting strength where comfort once lived.

Though her years were few, Linnie Bersheba Meadows Bryan left behind a legacy measured not in length of life, but in depth of influence. Her strength lived on through her daughter, carried forward into the Anderson family line, and preserved now through memory and record.

Linnie represents countless women whose lives were essential, whose sacrifices were unseen, and whose names deserve remembrance. Her story, once quiet, now stands where it belongs—within the enduring legacy of family.

List of children:

Joseph Calvin Bryan

A Son Who Remained Rooted

Joseph Calvin Bryan was born on **November 6, 1874**, in **Coffee County, Tennessee**, into a family grounded in land, labor, and tradition. As the son of **James Winton Bryan** and **Linnie Bersheba Meadows**, Joseph came of age in the familiar rhythms of rural

Tennessee life—where work began early, responsibilities were shared, and family bonds were formed through daily effort rather than ceremony.

Joseph's childhood unfolded during a period of transition in the South, as families rebuilt and adjusted in the decades following the Civil War. Like many young men of his generation, he learned his values not through formal instruction, but through example—watching his parents work the land, tend the home, and face hardship with quiet resolve.

The loss of his mother in **1898**, when Joseph was in his early twenties, marked a significant turning point for the Bryan family. Such losses were deeply felt, even if seldom spoken of. From that point forward, Joseph's life reflected the steadiness of someone shaped by responsibility and endurance rather than ambition or outward recognition.

Unlike some family members whose lives carried them westward, Joseph remained closely tied to **Coffee County**, choosing continuity over movement. His decision to stay rooted reflects a common but often overlooked strength—the ability to sustain family presence across generations in the same place, preserving memory, land, and local connection.

Joseph Calvin Bryan lived out his years in the county of his birth. He passed away on **December 7, 1950**, in **Coffee County, Tennessee**, closing a life that spanned seventy-six years. Though his story does not echo loudly through records, it lives quietly within the Bryan–Meadows family legacy.

His life stands as a reminder that not every legacy is marked by migration or public distinction. Some are marked by constancy—by remaining, by holding ground, and by ensuring that family roots stayed firmly planted in the Tennessee soil that first shaped them.

Betty Kate Bryan

Life Bridging Two Tennessee Counties

Betty Kate Bryan was born on **March 12, 1876**, in **Coffee County, Tennessee**, into the household of **James Winton Bryan** and **Linnie Bersheba Meadows**. Her early years unfolded in the familiar setting of Middle Tennessee, where families were connected to land, church, and kin, and where daughters often became the quiet backbone of family continuity.

Growing up in the years following Reconstruction, Betty Kate experienced a world shaped by change and endurance. Like many girls of her generation, she would have learned the skills essential to sustaining family life, managing a home, caring for others, and contributing to the daily work that held households together. These lessons, though rarely recorded, formed the foundation of a life lived in service and steadiness.

As adulthood unfolded, Betty Kate's life remained centered in Tennessee. Her journey eventually carried her into **Grundy County**, linking her story to the mountainous region where her mother, Linnie Bersheba Meadows, had been born. In this way, Betty Kate's life bridged the two counties that shaped the Bryan–Meadows line—Coffee and Grundy—connecting maternal and paternal roots through lived experience.

Betty Kate Bryan lived a long life, witnessing the passage of a century of change. She passed away on **January 29, 1972**, in **Tracy City, Grundy County, Tennessee**, at the age of ninety-five. Her years spanned eras of transformation, yet her life remained grounded in the same values that shaped her childhood.

Though records may list her only in dates and locations, Betty Kate's true legacy lived in family, continuity, and presence. She represents the strength of women whose lives were defined not by movement across great distances, but by the ability to hold family history steady across generations and place

Milton L. Bryan

A Life Brief, Yet Remembered

Milton L. Bryan was born on **March 19, 1878**, in **Coffee County, Tennessee**, the son of **James Winton Bryan** and **Linnie Bersheba Meadows**. He entered a household already shaped by hard work, close family ties, and the steady rhythms of rural Tennessee life.

Milton's childhood unfolded alongside his siblings during a time when family bonds were strong and daily life required shared responsibility. Like other children of his generation, he would have grown up close to the land—learning by observation rather than instruction, shaped by the presence of parents and older siblings who modeled endurance and duty.

Tragically, Milton's life was cut short. He passed away on **September 7, 1903**, at just **twenty-five years of age**. His death came only a few years after the loss of his mother, Linnie, and during a period when the Bryan family was still carrying the weight of that earlier sorrow. Such losses, while common in the era, were no less deeply felt.

Though Milton did not live long enough to leave behind a household of his own or a long trail of records, his place within the Bryan–Meadows family remains secure. He represents those family members whose lives ended quietly and early—yet whose existence mattered deeply to those who knew them and whose memory deserves preservation.

Milton L. Bryan's brief life reminds us that legacy is not measured by length of years alone. It is measured by belonging—by being part of a family's story, carried forward in remembrance, and honored by being named and remembered.

David Winton Bryan

A Brother Bound to Family and Place

102

Tags:

- Son of **James Winton Bryan** & **Linnie Bersheba Meadows**
- **Brother of Minnie May Bryan Anderson**
- **Brother-in-law of a great granduncle** *(by marriage into the extended Anderson line)*

David Winton Bryan was born on **March 22, 1882**, in **Asbury, Coffee County, Tennessee**, into a family already well rooted in Middle Tennessee soil. He was the son of **James Winton Bryan** and **Linnie Bersheba Meadows**, and a younger sibling within the Bryan household—growing up among siblings shaped by shared work, shared loss, and shared responsibility.

David's early years unfolded in the familiar setting of rural Coffee County, where families were closely knit and life revolved around land, labor, and kinship. As with many children of his generation, his upbringing would have been marked by early responsibility and a keen sense of belonging to both family and community.

The death of his mother in **1898**, when David was still a teenager, was a defining event for the Bryan children. That loss left an imprint on the family that carried forward into adulthood, shaping bonds between siblings who learned to rely on one another in the absence of a mother's presence.

David remained closely tied to Coffee County throughout his life. Unlike some relatives whose paths carried them westward, his story stayed rooted in Tennessee—reflecting the steadiness and continuity that characterized much of the Bryan–Meadows line. His life also connected him by marriage into the extended Anderson family network, establishing his place as a **brother-in-law within the broader Anderson lineage**, a relationship remembered within family tradition.

On **February 10, 1923**, David Winton Bryan passed away in **Ninth Model, Coffee County, Tennessee**, at the age of forty. Though his life was shorter than many of his siblings, his place within the family remains secure defined by kinship, shared history, and connection to the land that shaped him.

David's legacy lives not in distant migration or public record, but in family ties—brother, uncle, in-law—and in the quiet continuity of those who remained close to home.

James Walter Bryan

Life Spent Close to Home

Tags:

- Son of **James Winton Bryan** & **Linnie Bersheba Meadows**
- Brother of **Joseph Calvin Bryan, Betty Kate Bryan, Milton L. Bryan, David Winton Bryan**, and **Minnie May Bryan Anderson**

James Walter Bryan was born on **January 19, 1883**, in **Tennessee**, during the final years of the nineteenth century—a period marked by both hardship and resilience for rural families. He entered a household already shaped by responsibility, shared labor, and strong family ties, growing up alongside siblings who would each carry the Bryan–Meadows legacy in their own ways.

James's childhood unfolded in **Coffee County**, where family and place were deeply intertwined. Like many children of his generation, he learned early that life required steadiness and perseverance. The land and the people who worked it shaped his sense of identity, anchoring him to the community in which he was raised.

The loss of his mother, **Linnie Bersheba Meadows**, in **1898**, came when James was just fifteen years old. That early loss left an impression, shaping the character of the Bryan siblings as they matured in a household forever changed. Responsibility and self-reliance became necessities rather than choices.

Unlike some members of the extended family whose paths led far from Tennessee, James Walter Bryan remained close to his roots. His life continued in **Asbury, Coffee County**, reflecting a deep connection to the place where he was born and raised. His years were lived within the same landscapes that had shaped his parents and grandparents, preserving continuity within the Bryan line.

James Walter Bryan passed away on **March 10, 1967**, in **Asbury, Coffee County, Tennessee**, at the age of eighty-four. His life stands as a testament to those who carried family legacy not through movement or notoriety, but through constancy—remaining, remembering, and holding family history steady across generations.

Este: far top right corner.

Mary Estelle Bryan

A Daughter of the Bryan–Meadows Home

Tags:

- Daughter of **James Winton Bryan** & **Linnie Bersheba**

  Meadows

- Sister of **Joseph Calvin Bryan, Betty Kate Bryan,**
Milton L.

  Bryan, David Winton Bryan, James Walter Bryan, and

  Minnie May Bryan Anderson

Mary Estelle Bryan was born on **October 6, 1884**, in **Coffee County, Tennessee**, into a household already shaped by work, family responsibility, and the steady rhythm of rural life. As one of the younger children of **James Winton Bryan** and **Linnie Bersheba Meadows**, Mary grew up surrounded by siblings whose lives would unfold along both familiar and divergent paths.

Her early years were rooted in Middle Tennessee, where daughters often carried an unspoken strength within the family—helping maintain the home, supporting younger siblings, and learning the quiet disciplines that sustained households through changing times. Mary's childhood, like that of her siblings, was marked by closeness to family and place.

The death of her mother in **1898**, when Mary was just thirteen years old, marked a defining moment in her youth. Such a loss reshaped the Bryan family, leaving lasting impressions on the children who carried that absence into adulthood. Mary, like her siblings, learned resilience early, shaped by circumstance rather than choice.

Mary Estelle Bryan lived into the later decades of the twentieth century, witnessing immense change across her lifetime—from the world of her parents' generation to a modern era transformed by time and progress. She passed away on **March 18, 1967**, closing a life that bridged tradition and transition.

Though her story may appear quietly in records, Mary's place within the Bryan–Meadows family is secure. She represents the daughters whose lives sustained family continuity through presence, care, and connection—threads woven quietly but firmly into the larger family legacy.

William Whitson Bryan

A Son of the Later Years

Tags:

- Son of **James Winton Bryan** & **Linnie Bersheba Meadows**
- Brother of **Joseph Calvin Bryan**, **Betty Kate Bryan**, **Milton L. Bryan**, **David Winton Bryan**, **James Walter Bryan**, **Mary Estelle Bryan**, and **Minnie May Bryan Anderson**

William Whitson Bryan was born on **February 8, 1886**, in **Coffee County, Tennessee**, during the later years of the Bryan–Meadows

111

household. He entered a family already shaped by responsibility, shared labor, and the deep ties that bound parents and siblings together in rural Middle Tennessee.

As one of the younger children, William grew up in a home where older siblings had already begun stepping into adult roles. His early years were marked by the familiar rhythms of Tennessee life—family, land, and community—along with the quiet expectations placed upon children to contribute and endure.

The death of his mother, **Linnie Bersheba Meadows**, in **1898**, occurred when William was just twelve years old. That loss, coming so early in his life, left a lasting imprint on his childhood and shaped the path he carried forward. Like his siblings, William matured in a household forever changed, where resilience became a shared family trait.

William Whitson Bryan lived his life rooted in **Tennessee**, remaining close to the land and people that had shaped him from birth. His years spanned a time of tremendous change—from the rural world of his childhood to the modern age—yet his life remained grounded in familiar places and enduring values.

He passed away on **August 31, 1961**, in **Tennessee**, closing a life of seventy-five years. William's legacy rests not in grand movement or public record, but in continuity—one more life woven into the steady fabric of the Bryan–Meadows family story.

Aug. 1923 Hollister, CA. Minnie Bryan

Minnie May Bryan

The Daughter Who Carried the Line West

Tags:

- Daughter of **James Winton Bryan** & **Linnie Bersheba**

  Meadows

- Sister of **Joseph Calvin Bryan**, **Betty Kate Bryan**, **Milton L. Bryan**, **David Winton Bryan**, **James Walter Bryan**, **Mary Estelle Bryan**, and **William Whitson Bryan**
- Later wife of **John Watson Anderson**

Minnie May Bryan was born on **May 1, 1888**, in **Hillsboro, Coffee County, Tennessee**, the youngest daughter of **James Winton Bryan** and **Linnie Bersheba Meadows**. She entered a household already full of siblings, responsibility, and the quiet strength that defined the Bryan–Meadows family.

Minnie's childhood was shaped early by loss. In **1898**, when Minnie was just nine years old, her mother, Linnie, passed away. That absence marked her formative years, leaving Minnie to grow into adulthood within a family that had learned resilience through hardship. Like her siblings, she matured quickly, shaped by circumstance rather than choice.

As a young woman, Minnie's life followed a different path from many of her siblings. On **November 13, 1908**, in **Coffee County, Tennessee**, she married **John Watson Anderson**, joining the Bryan–Meadows line with the long-established Anderson family. Through that union, Minnie became the bridge between two family legacies.

Unlike most of her siblings who remained in Tennessee, Minnie's life carried her far from the land of her birth. She traveled west with her family, eventually settling in **Hollister, San Benito County, California**. Her journey reflects a broader pattern of migration seen in the early twentieth century—families carrying their roots across the country while preserving identity through memory and kinship.

Minnie May Bryan Anderson passed away on **March 8, 1967**, in **Hollister, California**. Her life completed a full arc—from Tennessee birth to California rest—carrying with it the legacy of her parents, her siblings, and the family she helped build.

Within the Bryan–Meadows family, Minnie stands as the daughter who carried their story beyond Tennessee's borders, ensuring that the family's roots extended westward while remaining firmly grounded in the past.

Jesse Thurman Bryan

I called him Daddy Thurm, but really, he was my step-grandfather, my grandfather on the Anderson side had already passed before I was born, my mother's father did not live here, here lived in Ohio, so Daddy Thurm is all I knew him as. I went to his funeral. Mom let me stay out of school to go. Thought the world of him, still do. BKA

A Son Who Returned Home

Tags:

- Son of **James Winton Bryan** & **Linnie Bersheba Meadows**

- Brother of **Joseph Calvin Bryan**, **Betty Kate Bryan**, **Milton L. Bryan**, **David Winton Bryan**, **James Walter Bryan**, **Mary Estelle Bryan**, **William Whitson Bryan**, and **Minnie May Bryan Anderson**

- **Brother-in-law of a great grand uncle** *(by marriage into the extended Anderson family line)*

Jesse Thurman Bryan was born on **September 12, 1892**, in **Hillsboro, Coffee County, Tennessee**, during the later years of the Bryan–Meadows household. He grew up in a family already shaped by shared responsibility, strong sibling bonds, and the quiet endurance required of rural Tennessee families at the turn of the twentieth century.

Jesse's childhood followed a period of profound change within the family. His mother, **Linnie Bersheba Meadows**, passed away in **1898**, when Jesse was just six years old. That early loss left a lasting imprint, shaping a childhood marked by resilience and the guidance of older siblings who helped steady the household in her absence.

Unlike some of his relatives whose lives carried them far from their birthplace, Jesse's story remained closely tied to **Hillsboro**. His life reflects a pattern seen throughout the Bryan family—movement through time rather than distance, rooted in the same community that had shaped generations before him.

Through marriage connections, Jesse also became linked to the broader Anderson family network, remembered as a **brother-in-law within the extended Anderson lineage**. These ties strengthened the bonds between the Bryan and Anderson families, reinforcing the interconnected nature of family history in Coffee County.

Jesse Thurman Bryan lived a long life, spanning more than eight decades of change. He passed away on **October 24, 1973**, in **Hillsboro, Coffee County, Tennessee**, closing a life that had begun and ended in the same community. His story stands as one of continuity—of remaining close to home, carrying family memory forward, and anchoring legacy through presence rather than movement.

Infant Bryan

Life Remembered, Though Brief

Tags:

- Child of **James Winton Bryan** & **Linnie Bersheba Meadows**
- Sibling of the Bryan children
- Died in infancy

Infant Bryan was born on **August 20, 1895**, in **Coffee County, Tennessee**, into the household of **James Winton Bryan** and **Linnie Bersheba Meadows**. Though life granted only a short span of days, this child's place within the Bryan–Meadows family is no less real or deserving of remembrance.

Infant mortality was a sorrow known all too well to families of the late nineteenth century. Loss came quietly and often, leaving grief carried inward rather than speaking aloud. For the Bryan family, this brief life would have been held in the same hopes and love given to every dream formed even before a future could unfold.

On **October 5, 1895**, Infant Bryan passed away in **Coffee County**, just weeks after birth. No records tell of personality or milestones, yet the simple fact of existence marks a place in the family story that cannot be erased.

In preserving this name, however brief the span of life, the family honors a truth long understood by those who came before us:

that every life matters,

that every child is part of the lineage,

and that remembrance itself is a form of legacy.

Leah Rhea Bryan

A Later Generation, Rooted in Tennessee

Tags:

- Member of the extended **Bryan family line**

- **Sister-in-law of a great-granduncle** *(by marriage into the Bryan–Anderson family network)*

Lennie Rhea Bryan was born on **March 12, 1922**, in **Tennessee**, into a generation that inherited the legacy of families already shaped by hardship, migration, and endurance. She entered life decades after the earliest Bryan siblings, during a period when the world was changing rapidly, yet family ties in rural Tennessee remained strong.

Her life unfolded primarily in **Coffee County**, a place deeply woven into the Bryan family story. While earlier generations carried the family name through loss, rebuilding, and westward movement, Lennie's years reflected continuity—remaining close to home and community, where family relationships continued to define daily life.

Through marriage, Lennie became connected to the extended Anderson lineage, remembered within family context as a **sister-in-law of a great granduncle**. These connections illustrate how family lines intertwine over generations, creating bonds that extend beyond direct descent and into shared history and kinship.

Lennie Rhea Bryan lived a full life spanning much of the twentieth century. She passed away on **July 22, 2000**, in **Coffee County, Tennessee**, closing a life that both inherited and sustained the family legacy passed down before her.

Though she belongs to a later generation, Lennie's place within the Bryan family record is secure. Her life stands as part of the living thread that connects the early Bryan–Meadows household to the present—proof that legacy is carried not only through ancestors, but through those who continue the family story forward in time.

Jay, Uncle George and Bennett boy on
top of Big Butt Mt.

Wade, Uncle George, and Bennett Boy on top
of Big Butt Mt. Having a taste LOL

Jay, Uncle George, Bennett Boy, Top of Big Butt

Edgar and Harriett Anderson, brother to John
Watson Anderson

Index

Anderson, Alva Lee

daughter of John Watson Anderson and Minnie Bryan..... 21-22

Anderson, Barbara Jo

family memories and recollections 37- 40

Anderson, Brian Keith

author reflections and family narrative 41-45

Anderson, Edgar

brother of Nathaniel Hamilton Anderson........................... 63-65

Anderson, Jay (John W. "Jay")

son of John Watson Anderson and Minnie Bryan 23-25

Anderson, John Watson (1884–1961)

birth and early life 8-9

marriage to Minnie May Bryan.. 9-11

migration west... 17-19

later years and burial 18-19

Anderson, Luther Nathaniel Tennessee

branch... 71-73

Anderson, Nathaniel Hamilton father of John Watson

Anderson 56-59, 79

Anderson, Sally Adelaide Horton mother of John

Watson Anderson.. 57-59

Anderson, Wade Buford children and

marriages 26-33

Anderson, Wade Buford Jr. son of Wade Buford

Anderson 32-33

Bryan, Betty Kate

daughter of James Winton Bryan.................................97

Bryan, David Winton brother of Minnie

May Bryan...102

Bryan, James Walter

son of James Winton Bryan
.............105

Bryan, James Winton

father of Minnie May Bryan 87-
90

Bryan, Jesse Thurman

brother of Minnie May Bryan......117

Bryan, Joseph Calvin

son of James Winton Bryan 94-
96

Bryan, Minnie May (1888–1967)

marriage and family

migration west........... 10-11, 17-19, 84-86

Bryan, Milton L.

son of James Winton Bryan...........99

Bryan, William Whitson

son of James Winton Bryan...........111

Gibson, Geniel Lee Anderson family

memories 34-36

Hannah, Edna Lola

second wife of Wade Buford Anderson 30-33

Leduc, Edna R.

first wife of Wade Buford Anderson.......... 27-30

Meadows, Linnie Bersheba mother of

Minnie May Bryan 91-94

California

Hollister 18-19, 26, 32, 44-45, 75-76, 84-86

San Benito County 18, 26-33, 84-96

Tennessee

Coffee County 8-11, 17, 56-59, 84-96

Hillsboro 8-11, 17, 56-59, 84-96